Unique You

Written by Lauren Duenas

Illustrations by Brooke Duenas

You are unique, yes it is true.

You are unique, there is only one you.

You are unique with your own talent and skill.

You are unique with every smile, giggle, and thrill.

You are unique, no matter your color.

You are unique if you have a sister or brother.

You are unique, whether you have one parent or two.

You are unique if you have a blended family that is new.

You are unique if you have special needs.

You are unique if it is hard to write or if you can perfectly read.

ABC

You are unique, whether or not you can talk.

You are unique, whether you use a wheelchair or walk.

You are unique, whether you are old or young.

You are unique like every story told or song sung.

You are unique, whether you have glasses or perfect sight.

You are unique with every ounce of your being and might.

You are unique, whether you are a girl or boy.

You are unique if not identifying brings you joy.

You are unique, whether you are short or tall.

You are unique, every bit of you and all.

You are unique, whether you are healthy or sick.

You are unique, whether you run slowly or quick.

You are unique, this will always be so.

You are unique, no matter how much you grow.

You are unique with each freckle and dot.

You are unique, don't let anyone tell you that you're not.

About the Author and Illustrator

We love celebrating everyone's individuality and what makes them unique! We are Disney fanatics, Starbucks regulars, beach goers, baking queens, singing partners, and the best bonus mom and daughter duo.

www.ingramcontent.com/pod-product-compliance
Lightning Source LLC
LaVergne TN
LVHW021353160826
845679LV00008B/1610

* 9 7 9 8 8 4 6 4 4 3 5 1 8 *